JIM McMAHON

★★★★★★★★★★★

MARCUS ALLEN

Jordan Deutsch

AVON SUPERSTARS

AVON BOOKS
A division of
The Hearst Corporation
1790 Broadway
New York, New York 10019

Copyright © 1986 by Avon Books
Published by arrangement with the author
ISBN: 0-380-75227-1

First Avon Printing: September 1986

AVON TRADEMARK REG. U. S. PAT. OFF. AND IN OTHER COUNTRIES,
MARCA REGISTRADA, HECHO EN U.S.A.

Printed in the U.S.A.

OPM   10   9   8   7   6   5   4   3   2   1

The author wishes to acknowledge the following:

The Football Hall of Fame
Inside Sports magazine
Sports Illustrated magazine
The Sporting News
Football Digest
Rolling Stone magazine
Chris Cobbs, from his work *Marcus Allen: Super Raider*

JIM McMAHON

Preface

McMahon... McMagic... McNificent

Jim McMahon is one of the very best players in the National Football League and certainly its most colorful and interesting personality. Pro football's newest sensation comes complete with sunglasses, a punk hairdo, and a style so original that writers from coast to coast are still looking for the right words to describe him.

Jim McMahon, the quarterback of the Chicago Bears, helped lead the Bears to an almost flawless 15–1 1985 NFL season and then on to the championship in Super Bowl XX in New Orleans. But any comparison between Jim McMahon and other football players, pro or otherwise, ends with the mere mention of his name. In fact, there is no athlete in any sport in the country—wrestling included—who comes close to fitting the unique style of McMahon.

Bears coach Mike Ditka describes him as "different."

Bears tackle Keith Van Horne says "crazy."

Bears receiver Dennis McKinnon calls him "a great leader."

Best friend and former college teammate Dan Plater uses the term "wild."

Keep on asking for a definition and you keep on getting different answers. Maybe because Jim Mc-

Mahon is not one "thing," but a different and refreshing human being. And if you ask Jim McMahon how he best describes himself, he'll tell you, "Be alert at all times—you never know what he's going to do. I don't even know what I'm going to do half the time."

But for the man who brought new life into the hearts of Chicago football fans and started a national fad by defying the orders of pro football Commissioner Pete Rozelle, there is much more to Jim McMahon than meets the eye. His road to success and the way in which he traveled it can't be found on any map in any atlas in the world.

It might be that Jim McMahon makes it up as he goes along, but chances are there's a "top secret" blueprint hidden away somewhere with a simple label that says, "Win, win, win; but have a good time while you are doing it."

1

Some Special Gifts for Grandma

James Robert McMahon was born on August 21, 1959, in Jersey City. But neither New Jersey nor San Jose, California, where his father, an accountant, moved the family when Jim was three, would ever get to claim much credit for having fostered such a famous son. That credit would go to Roy, Utah. That's where his parents, Jim and Roberta, and three sisters and two brothers made their way before Jim's sophomore year in high school.

For Jim, who lived in the poor section of San Jose before moving to Utah, his one shining memory turned out to provide him with a trademark in later life. It was there, when he was six, that he tried to use a fork to untie a knot on his toy cowboy holster. The fork slipped and went into his eye. As a result of the injury, he became sensitive to strong light and had to wear sunglasses.

But while Jim's days in San Jose may not have been his favorite time, his greatest fan remembers them well. That is his grandmother, Florence McMahon. For the 71-year-old grandmother of pro football's newest hero, visiting Jim and his family was a special occasion. As she says, "Every time I went there, he gave me something to remember him by."

On one visit she received a pink plastic gumball

machine ring, and on another a statue of the Blessed Virgin. When she told Jim that she felt he should keep the statue, he got very upset. "He thought I didn't want to take it," she said. "Tears just rolled down his face." Of course she still has the statue, along with the ring, which she still wears, and several other tokens of her grandson's early childhood "treasures." One of them happens to be a Christmas card which Jim received from his catechism teacher when he was an eight-year-old student in a San Jose Catholic school. What Jim did was to cross out his teacher's name and substitute his own. Inside the card he added this message: "This card is from my cathechism teacher. And I want to send it to you because you very nice when it was my birthday. You send me lots of money."

But her favorite gift from Jim was a six-inch statue he gave to her when he was eleven. It is of a boy, holding a hat between his legs, who has a smile that is innocent and yet mischievous. On the base of the statue is written: "I wish I could say what I feel."

To Grandmother McMahon there is no need for Jim to express more than he has over the years. She not only saves all the articles ever written about him, but watches him on television and attends games on the East Coast when she can. At the recent Super Bowl, she was her grandson's guest of honor.

For Jim, who was determined to do things his own way from his earliest years, growing up was not without its ups and downs. For a boy with too much energy to burn, it seemed that the answer was sports. He took to it all: football, baseball, and basketball. And he was strongly supported by his parents. As his father said, "If you want to do it, you can do it."

That seemed to become Jim's motto and, as his grandmother says, "He was always determined that whatever he did, he would win." The other residents of Roy, Utah, were the first to discover this attitude. To get on the starting football team he had to beat out two older quarterbacks, who just happened to be playing the position Jim wanted to play. He not only excelled on the football field, but also went on to make his mark in basketball and baseball—where he played every position but catcher. And more than once, he played in heroic style. In a state tournament baseball game he came up in the ninth with one out and the bases loaded. His team was down by four runs. He drove the first pitch over the left-field fence for a grand slam and tied the game! Earlier, in an important basketball game with his team down by one point and five seconds left on the clock, he stole the inbounds pass and scored the winning basket. Jim also played golf, but it is the one game he has yet to master.

But when the college scholarship offers came in, however, he was disappointed to find that Notre Dame, the school of his choice, was not interested in him. He had yet to reach his playing weight of today (which is roughly 187) and was considered too small. There were plenty of basketball offers, but he was determined to play a professional sport and he knew that a six-foot guard didn't stand much of a chance. He even had a shot at baseball, but as he said, "I finally gave that up because baseball players never seem to be at home, and I knew I would want to have a family someday."

The one offer he did take was from a college that wasn't too far away and had a football team that relied on its passing game. It was Brigham Young University in Provo, Utah. But as Jim was to learn, it may not have been his best choice. BYU is a strict school that likes its students to behave in a conservative and traditional way; but Jim was cut from a piece of cloth unlike any the school officials had ever seen. It was like trying to mix oil with water.

2

A Diet of Cherries

In the fall of 1977, 18-year-old Jim McMahon moved on from Roy, Utah, and its population of 17,000 to Provo, where Brigham Young University is located. The fact that Provo has a population more than triple that of his hometown of Roy didn't faze Jim in the least. The people it did affect were the crowds that watched him throw his long touchdowns and the school officials. They had no problem with the way he played on the field. It was his off-the-field performances that upset them.

When Jim played golf, his favorite pastime, he did it in his bare feet! When he wore shoes, they were the platform variety! Add to that his driving around town in a beat-up Dodge Charger and wearing a brown-and-white-checked polyester jacket. For the school, it was like having Huckleberry Finn enrolled on campus. Jim reminded a lot of people of the young Joe Namath, who just happens to be McMahon's boyhood hero and who went on to pro football's Hall of Fame. Like Jim, Namath not only won the big games and led the New York Jets to their only Super Bowl, an upset win over the then Baltimore Colts in 1969, but just happened to cause controversy every time he turned around.

But if Jim did not see eye to eye with the school

officials, he saw well enough to throw 75 touchdown passes during his junior and senior years alone! It was the kind of super performance which made him a consensus All-American. During the years of his leadership the team won the Western Athletic Conference every time and Jim wound up with an incredible 71 National Collegiate Athletic Association records. He even finished number three in the country in the voting for the famed Heisman Trophy award, placing just behind Marcus Allen and Herschel Walker. That, though, is not a popular subject with McMahon. He still believes that the school did not promote him enough because of his antics off the field.

There was even an incident on the field that caused as much embarrassment as some of Jim's other activities. The team was playing Southern Methodist University in the Holiday Bowl in 1980 and was down by 20 points, with only three minutes left in the game. Jim had the ball and was facing fourth down and 15 yards to go. The coach, LaVell Edwards, believing that the cause was hopeless, sent in the punting unit. What happened next is best described by Dan Plater, who was not only Jim's roommate but his favorite receiving target: "Jim came storming off [the field] and started yelling at the coach. He screamed: 'What are you doing? Quitting? Are you giving up?'" Coach Edwards would probably have liked to send Jim to the moon, but instead he let his brash quarterback go for broke and maybe even a miracle. Incredibly, Jim did lead his BYU teammates to 21 points and a 46–45 victory! Of course he won the MVP award for the game.

Jim carried the same attitude of winning on the field to everything else that he did. Plater, whom Jim still considers his best friend, tells a story about a table hockey game: "I beat him the first time, and he went off and practiced and practiced until he could beat me." Jim admits to throwing the hockey game all around Dan's house, but as he says, "I've never liked losing. I never could accept the fact that you have to lose, even though I know it's going to happen. I'm better at it now than I was [in college], but I don't like it. I never will like it."

Even his wife, Nancy, whom he met while at college, tells of Jim's determination to win. Of all things, it was over a backgammon game! "I got so I could beat Jim," said Nancy, "but he wouldn't quit until he'd won the last game of the night." A current teammate, Keith Van Horne, offensive tackle of the Bears, summed it up best by saying, "It doesn't matter what you're playing, racquetball, cards—he hates to lose more than anybody."

Of all the BYU memories, there is probably none that tops the summer when he decided to work for a farmer. But a day in the Utah heat having to clean out the animal stalls sent him into early retirement. With no money and no desire to return to the farm, he spent the summer sharing Plater's goodwill and living off the cherry tree in the backyard of their apartment building off the campus. As Jim describes it, "We ate cherry pie, cherry cobbler, raw cherries... Hey, you got hungry, you went to the backyard."

Having survived on a diet of cherries, Jim had only to survive the school. In spite of what he was told, he continued to play golf in his bare feet and pretty much do whatever else he wanted to do. Only Nancy had the influence to see him through. As Jim has admitted many times, "Nancy is the best thing that ever happened to me. I knew at BYU she was too good for me to lose. She helped me survive that place. She kept me alive....She put me right in my place, and now I'm not just taking up space. I'd be dead without her."

Of course Jim and Nancy weren't married in those days and she couldn't always be around to help him "survive." Once, in fact, after a game in Hawaii, Jim found that he was unable to sleep. So instead of going for a walk or to the lobby to buy a magazine, Jim decided to get some exercise by swinging from his hotel room's balcony, which just happened to be on the 24th floor! Not a recommended stunt. As Jim recalls, "I just climbed over our room's balcony and started swinging. My teammates told me I was going to kill myself, but I swung down to the twenty-third floor and knocked on the window to let me in." As luck would have it, the room was vacant and the balcony door locked. Jim just climbed back up. It's no wonder that Jim says, "Sometimes I wake up and realize I'm lucky to be alive."

Jim was now ready to bring his three-ring circus into pro football. As always, he was totally confident that come 1982 he would be wearing a pro jersey. If he had had his choice, it would have been the Los Angeles Raiders. Jim knew of their reputation as a team of individuals. It seemed just the place for him. But the Raiders were looking for a glamorous running back who had a national name. They were going to start the 1982 season in Los Angeles after spending their entire history in Oakland, and Marcus Allen, the Heisman winner out of the University of Southern California (which is located in Los Angeles), fit the bill perfectly. Quarterback was not their main concern.

Both of them were picked in the first round of the draft: Marcus was the tenth selection, and Jim was picked fifth by the Chicago Bears. The fact that he was still available when it came to the Bear's turn surprised head coach Mike Ditka and the rest of the Chicago front-office staff. And why not? The last time Chicago had a chance on a first-round quarterback draft pick had been 1951!

So Jim was on his way to the Windy City. But it was only a matter of time before the fans of Chicago would wonder who could kick up more wind, Jim McMahon or the weatherman.

The edge just might go to Jim.

3

Here Comes McMahon!

In 1982 the Chicago football world was ready for a
rebirth. Owner George Halas, also known as Papa Bear,
was one of the NFL's original founders and a former
star as well. He led the team in the 1930s when they
were known as the Monsters of the Midway, and now
wanted to restore the past glory of the Bears. To do
so he brought in a former Bear star, tight end Mike
Ditka, who was an All-Pro with the Bears in the 1960s,
and gave him the head coaching job. He also decided
to go for a young quarterback from Brigham Young
University. Halas knew what he was getting in Ditka,
but unfortunately he would never know exactly how
much he got in Jim McMahon. The following year the
"grandest Bear of them all" passed away.

Ditka hadn't yet met McMahon. As he waited in
Halas Hall, which is the training facility of the club,
with the other coaches, a limo was on its way from
O'Hare International Airport with the team's number
one draft pick. It was, of course, Jim McMahon. He
stepped out of the limo with his trademark sunglasses
and an attitude as casual as if he were stepping into
his own living room. Obviously for Ditka, who is more
like a father figure, seeing McMahon for the first time
was a unique experience. What was his reaction?

"There were no negatives. He was a different kind of guy, but you don't really know that until you meet him personally."

Ditka also didn't fail to notice the attitude. "I knew right then he wasn't out to impress anybody here...." When you ask Jim how he felt, if he was nervous or anything like that, he says, "No. I didn't see any reason to be. Somebody gets drafted number one every year." Ditka knew that better than most. After all, he had been the team's number one draft pick in 1961.

Both also shared a strong desire to win, but their ideas of how were very different. The Bears had always been known for their great defense. They also had the league's most respected running back in Walter Payton. Their game plan relied on keeping the score down on defense and controlling the line of scrimmage for Payton to run on offense. McMahon had always relied on his arm and a wide-open air game. Before Jim could finally get to pass on a steady basis he would have to prove himself all over again. His biggest problem in getting the Bears to change their plan of attack, though, was staying healthy.

That was something he found hard to do. But while he was able to escape serious injury in his rookie season of 1982, he couldn't do anything about the players' strike which wiped out almost half of the regular season. While the Bears limped to a 3–6–0 record, Jim had a good season. He completed 120 passes for 1,501 yards, threw for nine touchdowns, and ran for one. In 24 total attempts he ran for 105 yards, a nifty 4.4 average. He also managed to add a 59-yard punt to his record. Jim, it seemed, was not happy playing one position. It was something that Ditka was quickly learning. As he was to say later on, "The thing about Jim is he thinks he's our best passer, our best runner, our best blocker, our best tackler. And I'm serious. And I think he does it at his own speed, which is not good for a quarterback to do. He doesn't do anything halfway. And if you tell him, you're just going to be turned off."

In the next season the Bears moved to a respectable 8–8 record. After some early-season interceptions sent him to the bench, Jim was able to come on and put together a decent season. But as before, he didn't restrict his statistics to passing. He did get 2,184 yards in the air, but was more proud of his 307 yards on the ground and his three fumble recoveries! He did manage—in his "spare time"—to pass for 12 touchdowns, rush for two more, and catch an 18-yard pass for another.

What he was really beginning to accomplish, however, did not show up in the stats. His attitude and confidence were beginning to spread to his teammates. As Keith Van Horne said, "He's a catalyst, a spark. You see how how hard he plays the game, so you go and put out an extra effort." But while McMahon's style was endearing him to his teammates, some of his "go for broke" attitude was not pleasing Coach Ditka.

Believing that most rules to protect the quarterback should be abolished, Jim didn't wear the traditional "red shirt" in practice, the one that tells defensive players to "keep their hands off." As he says, "I don't like all the rules about you can't hit quarterbacks. Jack Lambert [the Pittsburgh Steelers' former defensive star] had the right idea when he said to put dresses on them all." He also had a special way of listening to what his coach said, such as the time Ditka wanted all players to wear shirts with collars on team flights. So what did Jim do? He put on a priest's shirt that had a collar but no back! Still, Ditka appreciates what McMahon's presence means to the team. As he says, "I tell you, where he goes, they go. They follow. He leads by saying: 'Hey, let's go. We're gonna take this hill over here, fellows.' He doesn't really say how. He just says: 'C'mon, we're gonna do it. I've got a plan.' Then he draws it in the mud and they go."

When wide receiver and teammate Ken Margerum describes McMahon and some of his habits, he sees the real purpose behind his quarterback's madcap antics: "He likes to be disgusting on purpose, just to get a reaction out of people. It gives him a special kind of mystique. I think that's healthy. It makes it hard for teams to read us. That's why he's a great quarterback. Defenses have the computer printouts of what you're going to do on first-and-ten and second-and-long and third-and-three, and Jim goes against all convention of what he's supposed to do. A lot of plays go to completely different receivers than the one that was planned. You can't defend that."

Off the field Jim was also making some headway. He and his wife, Nancy, whom he married in 1982, were living in a town house in suburban Chicago. It was Jim's wish that their first child be a girl. Sure enough it was. He and Nancy named her Ashley. Yet while he could be happy that his family had begun on a high note, he still had to prove to the football world that he was the same quarterback who had starred at BYU.

Maybe it would happen in 1984.

4
Buttin' Heads

Jim McMahon and the Chicago Bears opened the season with a 34–14 rout over Tampa Bay. It was the first time since 1979 that the team had won a season opener. They won their next game, against Denver, 27–0, but had a costly injury. Jim broke his hand during the game. He played a little in the next game, which the Bears won, 9–7, over Green Bay, but could not play against Seattle, where the team suffered a 38–9 setback. Then, when he finally returned on a full-time basis to lead the Bears to a 6–3 record, he ran into the tough hands of the Los Angeles Raiders and left the game with what turned out to be a lacerated kidney It not only ended his season but threatened to short-circuit his entire career, It was enough to make Jim stop and think about football: "When you're lying there in the hospital and they tell you they're going to give you an operation that could end your career, you gotta stop and think: 'What's going on here?'"

Ditka knew the answer was related to the fierce way his quarterback played the game: "I just wish he'd become more discreet, but the only thing he sees is the goal line or making a first down. He doesn't do it for show. He envisions himself as a winner and us as winners. He'll do anything he has to do to get it done.

A lot of quarterbacks wouldn't do that, and they shouldn't do it, because that's a position you can't afford to lose."

At the time of his injury, Jim was the league's top-ranked passer. He had completed 85 out of 143 passes for a 59.4 percent passing average. He had thrown for 1,146 yards and eight touchdowns. In the running department he had run up 276 yards on 39 carries for an impressive 7.1 average.

Although Ditka would rather that Jim be more careful and not get hurt as much, he also realizes what Jim's runs and scrambling mean for the team: "He has a great feel for the rush, and that's unique. A lot of quarterbacks never feel the rush, but he feels it, and he slides away from it. When you can do that with success, it becomes frustrating to the defense. They feel that if they've beaten their man, they've earned the right to tackle the quarterback. But all of a sudden, he's not there. He reminds me of [Fran] Tarkenton. He doesn't scramble for the sake of scrambling. He scrambles to make things happen, to find a receiver." Being compared to Fran Tarkenton, the holder of many all-time quarterback records, is quite an honor.

While Jim was recovering, the Bears held on to win the Central Division of the National Football Conference with a 10–6 record, their best showing in five years. Walter Payton, the Bears' All-Pro running back, finished the season with 1,684 rushing yards to bring his lifetime total to a remarkable 13,309 yards. It was enough to move him ahead of Hall of Famer Jim Brown and into first place on the all-time rushing list. But while Payton helped bring the Bears a 23–19 win in the divisional showdown with the Washington Redskins, he could do little in the NFC championship game against San Francisco. Without the threat of McMahon to throw the ball, the 49ers stacked the line of scrimmage with eight players to stop the run. Payton still managed to gain 92 yards but could not undo the 23–0 loss to the Super Bowl–bound 49ers. The one consolation for the Bears was getting to play in the championship game for the first time in 21 years!

The season itself also added another "McMahonism" to the growing list of famous firsts. The Bears' renegade quarterback came up with a unique new way to celebrate touchdowns. After a score, Jim would butt helmets with each of his linemen. Not lightly, but as Jim says, "We try to knock each other out." Ditka, of course, fearing injury, ordered the "butting" to stop. Jim pretended not to hear him, but when he went to his linemen to celebrate, they would just run away for fear of getting fined.

But they really never run that far from Jim. As a habit, he and the linemen go out for dinner every Thursday. In fact, his relationship with his linemen is unique by all football standards. Maybe that's because he wants to be one himself. As he is the first to admit, "Heck, if I was six-four and two hundred eighty, I'd be a lineman. I could have a good time doing that." Even the 280-pound offensive tackle Keith Van Horne, whom Jim likes to give an occasional piggyback ride to, says, "Our relationship with Jim is special. He likes to feel part of the line, and vice versa. It's different with other quarterbacks."

McMahon's view on the subject is also a practical one: "I've hung around with linemen since I was in high school. I appreciate what they do for me. Besides, you get one of those guys mad at you, and they can get you hurt in a hurry. All they have to do is pretend to slip and they could let a guy come right in on me."

The linemen are also his favorite target, and Jim will get them riled up whenever he can. As he tells it, "I'll come in the huddle and swear at them and they'll spit on me. The referees think we don't like each other, and sometimes I'll see the other teams looking at me like I'm crazy." But when you look at the results, that's the last thing Jim can be accused of. It's as he says: "We're different. We try and have fun out there."

Fun, McMahon style, sometimes means exchanging blows with your teammates. As was the case with roommate and guard Kurt Becker. It is one of the many kinds of stories which Jim is quick to tell: "Once when we were playing Tampa Bay, I was walking back to the huddle and all of a sudden, bam! Someone had belted me on the side of the head. I turned around and it was Becker, saying, 'Why don't you do something today?' So I kicked him."

As a final note to the year, the Bears rewarded Jim with a new contract putting him in the multimillion-aire's class with a five-year, five-million-dollar deal. It was a lot of money for the kid who started his trek in Jersey City, and for Nancy, too. But it didn't give either of them a swelled head. Nancy insisted that she would take care of Ashley and newly arrived Sean without outside help, and she also cleans and cooks without any professional help. And while they began planning their "dream house," Nancy still packed Jim's lunch for practice sessions in a leather briefcase. Typically, it consisted of two sandwiches plus Ding Dongs or Suzy Q's.

Jim might eat on the run, but it was the other 27 NFL teams that would have the stomachache in 1985.

5

A Year to Remember

The season of 1985 would be one of the brightest and most insane in the Chicago Bears' history and maybe in the history of the entire NFL. For openers, Jim McMahon came off the bench against Minnesota in a nationally televised night game and threw three touchdown passes in seven minutes to lead the Bears to a 33–24 win.

It was a remarkable performance. Jim had been on the sidelines because of not being able to practice due to a back injury that had him in traction a few days prior to the game. Jim's comment: "I finally got to play on national television."

While Jim was leading the Bears to victory after victory, he spent his free time with Nancy and the kids and listening to John Cougar Mellencamp, Bruce Springsteen, and Talking Heads. In between the victories, which included a "get-even-from-last-year" win over San Francisco, 26–10, and a 44–0 beating of Dallas—the worst defeat in Cowboy history—Jim reran a tape of Jack Nicholson in his favorite movie, *One Flew over the Cuckoo's Nest*, all the while sipping a Mountain Dew or a Classic Coke (which he did a commercial for with his linemen buddies) and nibbling a bowl of microwave popcorn. And why not? The Bears had gone through their regular schedule with a 15–1 record! It had been a truly great season, but Jim, of course, had suffered an injury that caused him to miss four games, including the loss to Miami on a Monday night game. Even with that one loss, a 38–24 affair to the Dolphins in Miami, the Bears had chalked up the best record in the NFL.

Jim and the team had certainly arrived in a big way. Of course he wasn't alone. Mike Ditka was the overwhelming choice for Coach of the Year honors; running back Walter Payton had established a new NFL record by rushing for 100 yards (or more) in nine straight games before being tied for the honor by the Raiders' Marcus Allen in the last week of the season; and the Bears had unveiled William ("The Refrigerator") Perry, the 305-pound defensive tackle who was put on offense in some special goal line situations and who scored some important touchdowns with his power-driving one-yard lunges and short catches as well as being a devastating blocker for Walter Payton and Matt Suhey. There was also the defense, the best in the league, led by All-Pros Dan Hampton, Mike Singletary, and Richard Dent. And there was also Buddy Ryan, the defensive coordinator and mastermind of the 46 defense.

But, of course, the season would not be complete without some Ditka–McMahon showdowns. The hottest of these involved practice and training films, things that Jim didn't think were necessary. As he said, "I've never enjoyed practice. Practice is practice. It's not a life-and-death situation. It's something you have to get through each week in order to get to Sunday. Sunday, that's show time. What's the use of having your best day on Tuesday? That's not gonna win you the game."

While Ditka would not allow his prized quarterback to miss practice, he gave a little when it came to watching the films in preparation for the next game: "His knowledge and his vision of what's going on seem to improve from game to game. He doesn't have to spend as much time with film as others. He's not like most quarterbacks. He probably is most unlike any other quarterback in the league, but that doesn't mean he's not more into the game than any other quarterback. Some guys look at film over and over. I think Jim looks at it once, and then he starts thinking. He sees it in his head more than he would see it on a screen. He sees situations flash, and then he says, 'If this happens, I do this. If this happens, I go this way.' I don't know if Jim's got eyes in the back of his head or what."

Up until the divisional playoff game against the New York Giants—which the Bears easily won, 21–0—Jim's "horseplay" had not caught the attention of the commissioner's office. But in that game Jim wore a headband which read *Adidas*. It was enough of a violation to allow Commissioner Pete Rozelle to slap a $5,000 fine on the Bears. The reason? Allowing Bears players to wear "advertising" as part of their uniform is against NFL rules.

So what does Jim do in the NFC championship game against the Los Angeles Rams a week later? Simple, he wears a headband that reads *Rozelle!* The Adidas headband is also there, but around his neck. Rozelle, realizing the humor of it, said, "A great gag." And there was no fine this time.

Everyone but the Rams was laughing. The Bears rolled to another playoff shutout, 24–0, as Jim led the attack with 16 of 25 passes for 164 yards while throwing for one touchdown and scampering for another on a 16-yard run. The Bears had the championship, their first since 1963! But of course Jim did not escape the game without tearing up his body once again. This time it was his backside, which he badly bruised while trying to slide for safety on one of his runs.

Considering that it marked the umpteenth time Jim

had found a way to get to the first-aid station—bad back, four knee operations, broken bones, tendinitis, muscle spasms, and the lacerated kidney—there should not have been any special fuss made over the latest mishap. After all, the only thing Jim wanted was for the Bears to bring Hiroshi Shiriashi, an acupuncturist, down to New Orleans to help get him ready for the Super Bowl and the New England Patriots. (An acupuncturist is someone who medically treats a patient with the use of needles to remove pain.) The Chicago management objected to the treatment.

When Jim insisted that the Bears bring in Shiriashi, everyone knew it was not going to be a dull Super Bowl. Maybe on the field, where the games were never really that exciting, but not off the field where Jim McMahon was about to begin his "Invasion of New Orleans."

6

Shufflin' toward the Super Bowl

It seems that wherever Jim McMahon goes something unexpected is bound to happen. When he and the Bears arrived in New Orleans a week prior to Super Bowl XX to take on the Patriots, the newspapers were still hot on the story of Hiroshi Shiriashi. Then, when the acupuncturist came to town to treat Jim's badly bruised buttock, the attention shifted to some comments about the people of New Orleans that a local sportscaster said Jim had made. Before the dust had a chance to settle, the people of New Orleans were ready to storm the gates of the Bears' training camp and hoist Jim up on the nearest flagpole. But, of course, when it became known that Jim had been falsely accused, things cooled off a bit.

When Jim wasn't under Shiriashi's needles, he was taking in the sights of the city's famous French Quarter. Everywhere Jim went he was mobbed by reporters who were always on the lookout for another headline, as well as hundreds of fans. After all, everything he was doing nowadays was news and sometimes even big business. His headband had inspired promoters to jump all over the idea and sell tens of thousands across the country. Among the other Bears souvenir items that were selling like hotcakes was a videotape of a song that he and some of the Bears made called

"The Super Bowl Shuffle." Some critics thought that making the tape before winning the Super Bowl might just spell trouble and prove a jinx. But as the Bears started moving toward the big event, sales went over the 100,000 mark.

As far as the game was concerned, the Bears were big favorites. There was even talk that they might shut down New England and become the first team ever to go through the playoffs and the Super Bowl without allowing a point on the scoreboard. Well, almost. The Patriots managed 10 points to the Bears' 46. More embarrassing to New England was their rushing attack. The Bears limited them to seven yards for a new Super Bowl record! Oddly enough, the Pats scored first on a field goal, and when the message board flashed that 15 of 19 teams that scored first won, All-Pro defenseman Mike Singletary said, "Yeah, but none of those fifteen ever played the Bears."

Jim started the first scoring drive for the Bears with a 60-yard strike to Willie Gault. And while he didn't throw for any touchdowns, he did complete 12 of 20 passes for 256 yards and did score twice himself. He left the game with the score 44–3 with 18½ minutes still to play. Yet, in or out of the game, Jim kept the crowd and the 100 million TV viewers on their seats with his show of headbands. Letters had come in from all over the country with suggestions, and Jim picked what he thought were the best. When asked how he arrived at such a cross section of headbands he said, "Because I have imagination."

Included was *JDF–CURE* for the Juvenile Diabetes Foundation, *POW–MIA* for Vietnam prisoners of war missing in action, *United Way, Support Children's Hospitals*, and *Pluto*, which was the most personal. Pluto is the nickname of Jim's former teammate at BYU, Danny Plater. Jim's best friend was undergoing treatment for a malignant brain tumor. The former BYU star was a fourth-round draft choice by the Denver

Broncos but had to abandon a football career because of the illness. While Plater was watching the game (he is in his second year of med school at USC) he saw the headband. Even though Jim had called earlier in the week and said he was going to wear it, Plater thought he was only messing around. When Jim told reporters after the game about "Pluto," he said, "He's had two operations in two years. And radiation. He's very lucky to be alive. I love him. The boy just keeps hanging on." Jim, by the way, also wore a headband that said I heart ["love"] N.O., as a gesture to the people of New Orleans.

While the game MVP honors went to defensive end Richard Dent for causing two fumbles and recording 1½ sacks while generally terrorizing the Pats' offense, Jim took satisfaction in the Bears' resounding victory. After the game Jim was floored by TV and movie offers which rolled in. MTV wanted him to be a guest video jockey. The A-Team wanted him for an appearance. Saturday Night Live wanted him to be a guest host, and Hollywood wanted him to tear up the big screen. But he refused them all, saying, "I hate acting." He did make an appearance on Miami Vice (who could blame him?) and also got invited to the Pro Bowl as the starting quarterback for the NFC.

Away from all the hype of the Super Bowl, there was the more serious side which did not get any headlines. Jim, for example, arranged to have an out-of-work steelworker and his wife flown in from Utah and set the couple up with a hotel and tickets. He bought a new bike for a poor boy after he learned his had been stolen. Most unnoticed by the bright lights of the TV cameras was a legless old man in a wheelchair who waited for the quarterback in a corridor under the stadium. When Jim heard a voice cry out, "Jim, please..." he turned around, walked back, leaned over, and embraced the man.

It was not a unique thing for Jim to do. Even with

his eye always on the goal line, his vision takes in a larger territory. Sharing that moment with the man in the wheelchair in the height of all the postgame turmoil only confirmed that, superhero or not, Jim McMahon has a keen sense of where the football field ends.

He also knew what the Super Bowl victory meant for the future, long after he hangs up his cleats and calls it a day. "In the end a good quarterback is a guy who won. Look at Terry Bradshaw. They said he'd never be great, but he won four Super Bowls. To me, he's probably the geatest just because of that. And Joe Willie [Namath]. He didn't have the greatest stats, but he won the Super Bowl, too. Then there's someone like Fran Tarkenton, with all the career records, yet he never won the big one. And he had the opportunities. He was a good quarterback, but it's wins and losses that count."

Following the Super Bowl, Jim went to Hawaii for the Pro Bowl. He started the game but had to leave because of an injury as the Giants' Phil Simms came on to take the game MVP honors in the win over the American Football Conference. Unlike the time in Hawaii when Jim couldn't sleep and was doing exercises by swinging from the 24th-floor balcony, he had his wife Nancy along for this trip. Jim, naturally, skipped any high-wire acrobatics. With the Super Bowl victory still hot news, there were, of course, many calls and many well-wishers. But none was more fitting than the gift from the Juvenile Diabetes Foundation. The gift was an elaborate flower arrangement with the note, "You will always be our hero. What more can we say?" Because of Jim's headband, *JDF–CURE*, the foundation reported receiving $30,000 in recent donations.

Finally, after four years which had his name in the injury column almost as often as in the box score, Jim had accomplished the ultimate goal—a Super Bowl win. And barring injuries, he might even have a chance to go on and catch Terry Bradshaw and earn three more championship rings. But whether he does or not, one thing is for certain: There's only one Jim Mc-Mahon. Or, as Danny Plater sums it up so well, "He doesn't mold his life after anybody, doesn't do what other people want him to do. Jim McMahon has grown up the way Jim McMahon has wanted to grow up. Maybe that's why he's happier than the rest of us."

"That's my boy": Jim McMahon and his father hug after Jim led Brigham Young University to a thrilling 38–36 victory over Southern Methodist University in the 1980 Holiday Bowl.
AP/Wide World Photos

Jim gets a rookie's rough introduction to the NFL as the
Minnesota Vikings sacked him seven times and beat the
Bears 35–7.
AP/Wide World Photos

Back on the bench, Jim looks like all of those sacks have
given him a large headache.
AP/Wide World Photos

Fading back and looking for a receiver and six points.
UPI/Bettmann Newsphotos

Jim is a picture of concentration as Super Bowl XX is about to begin. The headband "JDF Cure" stands for Juvenile Diabetes Fund, and Jim wore it to help raise money for the charity.

Jim celebrates a Bears' touchdown in the Super Bowl while looking for a head to butt.
AP/Wide World Photos

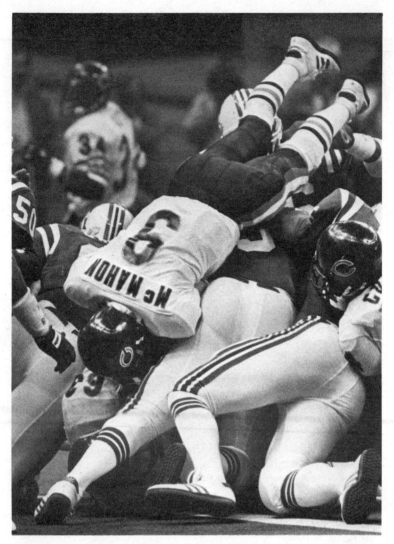

McMahon "uses his head" to score his second touchdown against New England.

Jim decides it is easier to cheer William "The Refrigerator"
Perry into the end zone.
UPI/Bettmann Newsphotos

Jim hugs his teammate and all-time NFL rushing leader, Walter Payton, after their victory in Super Bowl XX.
UPI/Bettmann Newsphotos

Marcus Allen is always stretching for extra yards. Here he is shown leading University of Southern California to a 41–17 victory with four touchdowns.
UPI/Bettmann Newsphotos

That extra effort earned Marcus the Heisman Trophy as the
best player in college football.
UPI/Bettmann Newsphotos

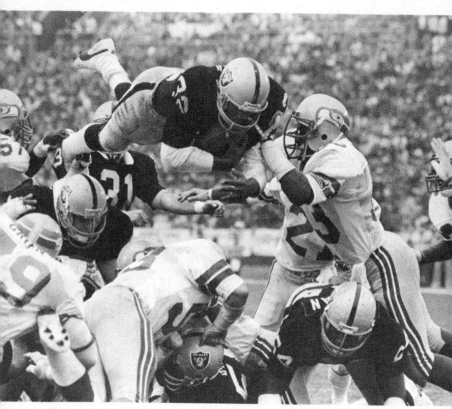

Marcus is airborne and headed for the end zone.
UPI/Bettmann Newsphotos

In Super Bowl XVIII, Marcus ran around the Redskins...
UPI/Bettmann Newsphotos

...And simply outran them.
UPI/Bettmann Newsphotos

Marcus's red-hot effort won him a cold day in New York
City, as well as a new car and the MVP Trophy.

Marcus breaks a tackle and scores three touchdowns against Miami.

A smiling Marcus Allen receives the Schick Trophy as the NFL's MVP in 1985.
AP/Wide World Photos

MARCUS ALLEN

Preface
Bound for Greatness

What Marcus Allen, star running back of the Los Angeles Raiders, has accomplished at the age of 25 is more than most athletes could ever hope for in two lifetimes. Or maybe three.

He was an All-American in high school and college and has already been an All-Pro twice. He has established records at every level that he has ever played and was the hero of Super Bowl XVIII.

In high school, he led his team to the city championship. In college, he won the Heisman Trophy as the most outstanding player in the country in 1982. And the following year he was the Rookie of the Year in the NFL, and then went on to be named the MVP of Super Bowl XVIII and then the Player of the Year in 1985.

And he has only just begun his professional career. What lies ahead for this brilliant football player can only be imagined. He is considered the offensive workhorse of the Raiders and is a threat to run, throw, or catch on any play. Ask him to make three yards and he'll try for ten. Ask him for ten and he'll find some way to reach the end zone.

When he's not running with the ball or going out to receive, he'll either be blocking for a teammate or taking a pitchout from the quarterback and passing.

And he has the uncanny ability to almost always be involved in the big play of the day, the one that wins the game.

Even now, with only four years of pro ball under his belt, he seems destined to wind up in the Hall of Fame. He is probably one of the few players to have ever had their high school football jersey number retired by the school!

But success, as Marcus will be the first to admit, did not come as easily as many people think. Many scouts thought that he was not big enough or fast enough to play pro ball. In college he had to wait his turn before becoming the regular ballcarrier, and in the pros he had to be patient with an offense that relied more on passing than running. But he hung in there, making the most of any opportunity when it was given to him. It is this trait of patience and perseverance that most probably makes Marcus Allen a very special player and an even more special person.

His is a truly unique story.

1

Growing Up

On March 26, 1960, the second of Red and Gwen Allen's six children was born. They named him Marcus LaMarr Allen. And as things turned out, their newly born son would not only be raised in San Diego, but go on to play all of his high school, college, and pro ball in the southern part of California. In fact, except for a brief skiing trip a few years back, Marcus had grown up without ever seeing snow.

From the beginning, things were not to be usual for Marcus. With his older brother getting his father's real name (Harold), his parents used the local phone book to come up with the name of Marcus. Following Marcus came Damon (who went on to play quarterback at Cal State University at Fullerton) and a set of fraternal twins, Michelle and Michael. The last of the children was named Darius.

Marcus and his brothers and sisters were all fortunate to live in a house which their father built (he was a building contractor) and grow up with a couple of Shetland ponies to ride in the vacant lot next door. They were also fortunate to have some professional medical help always around, as their mom, Gwen, was a registered nurse.

When Marcus began playing organized football at the age of ten, it was obvious that he was better than the other boys. But his dad, knowing the importance of keeping everything in balance, was quick to warn his athletic son, "Always remember there is going to be somebody else better than you."

Of course his dad's statement would eventually come true as Marcus kept on finding tougher and tougher competition to play against, but in the beginning that was not the case. On the Little League baseball team (which his father coached) Marcus was the star shortstop, and by the time he enrolled in Abraham Lincoln High School in southeast San Diego, his special athletic talents were already being talked about. He was not only the best player on a good football team at Lincoln, but excelled on defense as well as offense.

Aside from his performance on the field, Marcus also found the time to do well in his schoolwork and also get involved in club and extracurricular activities. He even learned to play the piano. But that took some urging by his dad, especially after it was discovered he had decided on his own to skip piano practice for a couple of months without telling his folks.

At Lincoln High School, Marcus was considered the most popular kid on campus. It was there that he got the first of his nicknames. Because his complexion was light, his friends called him Casper the Ghost. But the name might well have been given because of the way in which he tried to become invisible when it came to receiving the many awards he had earned. Marcus was never caught up with being a star athlete and wanted nothing more than to just blend in with his friends and teammates. As he often said to his high school football coach, Vic Player, "Aw, Coach, why me? Why not the rest of the guys, too?"

By the time Marcus became a senior at Lincoln, his reputation as an outstanding football player was becoming legend—at least on a local level. But with it came some problems. Coach Player wanted Marcus to play regularly in the quarterback position on offense in addition to his defensive chores. He knew that with all of Marcus's skills and leadership ability it would be just the right element to bring the team together and maybe win the city championship. But Marcus, with his eye on a possible pro career in the future, knew that his chances of being a successful black quarterback in the pros were slight. After all, there had never really been one before. To add to the problem, Marcus didn't like the idea of standing out in the crowd.

So, in practice, Marcus kept on fumbling the snap from the center. Coach Player realized that Marcus was trying to send a message that he was unhappy with his decision. But there was no way the coach was going to let one of his players—no matter who he was—show him up. It would have been disastrous for the team. So, in a fit of anger, he told Marcus to get off the field. Of course Marcus returned the next day, helmet in hand, and apologized. As the coach would later admit, there was no way he would have let Marcus quit the team. It was just his way of letting everyone know who was boss. For Marcus, it was a lesson that he would never forget and one which would have great benefits in the years to come.

That year, 1977, Marcus not only led his team to the city championship as a full-time quarterback with a 12–0–1 record, but racked up an incredible 1,434 yards and nine TDs passing, and 1,098 yards rushing to go along with 12 more TDs! He also starred on defense. When it came to the championship game against rival Kearny High School, he was a one-man wrecking crew. In the lopsided 34–6 victory he scored five touchdowns. Four of them came on runs of 85, 30, 20, and 10 yards, and the fifth on a 60-yard run with an interception!

That performance earned him a place on the *Parade* Magazine All-American High School Team and the Hertz (Rent-a-Car) Number 1 Award as the top high school athlete in California.

All that remained was picking a college of his choice.

2

2,000 Yards and the Heisman!

Offers from all the major colleges had poured into the Allen household. The most famous member of the Allen family was now ready to join a team that might make him even more famous. The fact that there was only one school for Marcus was a secret which his friends knew better than the college recruiters. As Marcus says, "It was always USC. Like every other kid in southern California, I grew up loving USC football and UCLA basketball. But I was going to play football—not basketball—so there was no choice."

Of course, University of Southern California football coach John Robinson, now head coach of the Los Angeles Rams, was not about to take any chances and let Marcus get away. The USC campus was 120 miles away from San Diego and in every sense of the word Marcus was a local "phenom."

When Robinson went to visit Marcus and his parents, he arrived to a full house. All of Marcus's brothers and sisters were there, and the mood was like a party. Then, suddenly, in the middle of the coach's talk, the lights went out! It was only a temporary power failure and not enough to end the visit. Marcus's mother, Gwen, got out some candles along with milk and cookies. It was an experience Robinson would never forget.

If Robinson's visit and Marcus's own boyhood dream weren't already enough to cinch his choosing USC, then meeting O. J. Simpson, Marcus's hero, would be the clincher. Simpson was not only the first and then only man to rush for 2,000 yards in one NFL season, but had won the award given to the best college player in the country when he won the Heisman Trophy in 1968 while a running back at USC.

Marcus met O.J. at the Hertz award banquet and they became instant friends. After all, they were both from California and both were incredible runners, although Marcus had a way to go before matching the exploits of his newly found friend.

When Marcus arrived at USC, he expected Coach Robinson to use him as a defensive back based on the way he had performed at Lincoln, taking down runners almost as fast as he had racked up yards and touchdowns. But four days after the practice season began, Robinson switched Marcus to tailback. It was a dream position, but in 1978 when the USC Trojans marched to the co–National Championship with Alabama, Marcus was only a freshman. He got to carry the ball only 31 times and turned in 171 yards. Still, it was an impressive 5.5 average per carry. And most important, Marcus got to score a touchdown.

But soon after the Trojans rolled over Ohio State in the Rose Bowl, Marcus was told by Robinson that he wanted to switch him from tailback to fullback. Marcus knew that being a fullback in the USC game plan meant being exclusively a blocker. It was a blow for an 18-year-old kid who had had his heart set on the glamour position at the top college in the country.

Robinson had seen that Marcus was hesitant, and he asked his young player what he thought of the decision, reminding Marcus that the tailback job belonged to Charles White, one of the leading rushers in the nation and a good choice for the Heisman Trophy. Of course Marcus's decision was to go along with his coach, and as Robinson said, "I knew Marcus was willful and had a strong personality. But I had no sense that Marcus would be difficult too deal with, and he wasn't. He was all a coach could hope for. A guy with ambition will do anything, and Marcus obviously had a lot of ambition."

The next season Marcus got a taste of fullback on his first fall practice when he threw a block and had his nose broken. But he quickly recovered and helped the Trojans have another sensational year. USC finished with an 11-0-1 season and another victory in the Rose Bowl over Ohio State, 17-16, but when it came to the National Championship it was given to Alabama. Still, Marcus's blocking and White's running (2,050 yards) were nothing to be unhappy about. White was named the Heisman Trophy winner, and Marcus gained 649 yards rushing and scored eight touchdowns in his backup position. He also showed his great versatility by catching 22 passes for a 14.3 average. As Coach Robinson said at the time, "Marcus is one of those guys you could hand a golf club for the first time, and he'd hit the ball right down the middle. Then he'd help you find your ball."

In the off-season, Marcus's friendship with O.J. continued to grow. He was even asked to house-sit while Simpson was away. Marcus gladly accepted, but in getting ready for his new role as the USC tailback in 1980 (Charles White had graduated and been drafted by the NFL's Cleveland Browns), he made the mistake of practicing indoors. When O.J. returned to find some broken furniture, he put in a new rule: "When Marcus stays at my house, he stays outside. He can play tennis, swim, whatever...I don't want him practicing broken-field running in my living room."

Marcus was now known as Young Juice, more for his similarity in style and poise to O.J. than for his furniture breaking. And he was ready to take on the tradition of USC tailbacks as the season of 1980 got under way. Before him had been three tailbacks who had all won the Heisman: Mike Garrett in 1965, Simpson in 1968, and White in 1979. There had also been Clarence Davis, Anthony Davis, and Ricky Bell, not to mention other backs and ends, including Frank Gifford, a Hall of Famer, and Lynn Swann, former star of the Pittsburgh Steelers. Interestingly enough, Marcus had known all the former USC tailbacks who won the Heisman. He had blocked for White, had a good friend in Simpson, and was given a lift one day after football practice while at Lincoln High School by Garrett. They didn't know each other, but Garrett had seen Marcus and couldn't resist giving a lift to "the kid in the dirty uniform."

Marcus was able to post some impressive stats in his first year as the regular tailback, but neither he nor the team could overcome the quarterback problems. While the Trojans finished the season at 8−2−1 (a so-so season for them), Marcus ran for 1,563 yards and 14 touchdowns (a *very* nice season for a running back). If he had one wish for the next season, his last in a Trojan uniform, it was to reach 2,000 yards rushing.

He did better than that, even though the Trojans improved just a little bit to finish at 9−2−0. Carrying the ball 433 times, he averaged 5.6 yards a carry and finished with an NCAA record of 2,427 yards! He also became the first player to rush for more than 200 yards in his first five games. In all, he had established 12 NCAA records and had a share of a 13th. That season, plus his overall college record, including bowls, of 4,810 yards on 932 carries caused Robinson to say, "Marcus Allen is the greatest football player I have ever seen."

Now, of course, was the question of the Heisman. Marcus had some stiff competition. There was Herschel Walker of Georgia, Jim McMahon of Brigham Young University, and Dan Marino of the University of Pittsburgh. When Simpson was asked about the Young Juice's chance, he said, "I think he can win the Heisman. He better, because I'm not about to lend him mine."

Simpson didn't have to. Marcus was named the Heisman winner in addition to being named the *Sporting News* College Player of the Year. He also collected a host of other honors. Still, with all the fanfare, some of the pro scouts didn't think he was big enough or fast enough to be a superstar in the pros. When it came to the draft, two other running backs, Darrin Nelson of Stanford and Gerald Riggs of Arizona, were chosen ahead of Marcus. Nelson went to the Minnesota Vikings and Riggs to the Atlanta Falcons. Marcus was taken tenth on the first round by the then Oakland Raiders.

The Raiders have always been considered the "outlaw" team of the NFL. And this reputation increased because Al Davis, who was one of the team's owners, was fighting the NFL and Commissioner Pete Rozelle in the courts for the right to move the Raiders to Los Angeles for the 1982 season. That, and the fact that the NFL was facing a players' strike, were some of Marcus's worries as he got ready to launch his pro career. What had to make him feel good, though, was the fact that Al Davis probably has the sharpest eye for talent in the entire NFL.

3

Rookie of the Year

When Marcus Allen played at USC he had wanted to wear number 32. It was that number that had belonged to his boyhood hero, Simpson. But with Simpson's exploits at USC in the 1960s, the school had retired the number. So Marcus wore number 33. Now, with the Raiders, he was presented with the jersey which read 32.

Considering the confused state the Raiders were in, it was one of the better greetings to life in the NFL, or, to be more exact, life with the Raiders. The team had made the move to Los Angeles in spite of what the league officials and other owners had said. It would be up to the courts to decide that question. But because of the uncertainty of where the Raiders would play in 1982, the only thing that had been established was that the team would use the 100,000-seat capacity of the L.A. Coliseum for their home games. No practice facility had been arranged, and Marcus and the other Raiders found themselves having to practice in their old home, Oakland, 400 miles away. That meant that players like Marcus would have to spend weekdays in a motel and then fly into L.A. on Friday or Saturday, or to whatever city was on the schedule.

For Marcus, who had just signed a four-year, one-million-dollar contract with the help of his agent, Ed

Hookstratten, it meant that he would be spending little time in the new home he had just bought in Los Angeles. Hookstratten, by the way, also represented Simpson, and Marcus had been staying in a guest room at O.J.'s house. So it seemed that O.J. really wasn't too upset about the furniture Marcus had broken. In fact, he often referred to Marcus as his "little brother" and also gave him another nickname. Because of Marcus's long neck and small eyes, O.J. thought that Allen resembled E.T., the famous alien of the Steven Spielberg movie. It was not a name Marcus was crazy about, and when anyone asked he would say it stood for "Extra Talented."

When Marcus arrived at the Raiders' training camp, which was in the northern California town of Santa Rosa, on July 22, 1982, he quickly saw why the players had called the place El Rancho Tropicana. The temperature was always in the 90s. For Marcus, switching from the cardinal and gold colors of the Trojans to the black and silver of the Raiders was a drastic turnaround. Even the Raiders' insignia—resembling a skull and crossbones—told him it was a different world. Here was an aggressive team of 45 different individuals, all led by the man considered to be the greatest maverick in pro football, Al Davis, an owner who dressed only in black and white and wore his hair in a 1950s style.

The Raiders were the kind of players who were impressed only with effort and honesty. They didn't care if Marcus had won a Heisman or not. But Marcus had no trouble quickly winning over coach Tom Flores and the rest of the players. As veteran guard Gene Upshaw has said, "He didn't try to set himself above everybody because he won the Heisman Trophy. Once he opened up and embraced us, it was almost immediate. We all liked him. He didn't come out of USC with a big head. I guarantee you that eight or nine years from now, you'll watch him and still think he's a rookie."

From Marcus's point of view, the Raiders and Al Davis from the inside were very different from what most people thought about them: "Al Davis is a great owner. He cares about his players. He takes in problem players and gives them a chance to play, and it has worked. We're individuals, we're not forty-five dress-alikes. I know that because I'm an individual, too. But I know when we run on the field, we're going to get booed sometimes. I can hear it now." Some people just don't like the Raiders' fierce image.

When the Raiders came into L.A. Coliseum for the first time as the Los Angeles Raiders, it was for their third exhibition game of the season. And Marcus, who had spent his college days playing in the Coliseum, was the first Raider to score a touchdown in their new home, helping his team defeat the Green Bay Packers, 24–3.

But that was part of the exhibition season. When play started for real, the Raiders were faced with the prospect of just having come off a disappointing 7–9 season and having to face the defending Super Bowl champion San Francisco 49ers. The fact that the Raiders were playing at home was no comfort, especially in the face of a new crowd of fans. But with Jim Plunkett at quarterback and Marcus and fullback Kenny King in the backfield, the Raiders stopped the 49ers 23–17. For Marcus, it was a sparkling debut. He gained 116 yards, the most for a Raiders back since 1977, and caught four passes for 64 yards. Even King, whom Marcus had replaced as the main running threat, had nothing but praise: "He takes off on a dime and wiggles past tackles. I'm not jealous of him. I'm just glad he's here."

In the next game, at Atlanta, Marcus showed some more of his unique ability by setting up a touchdown with a 47-yard pass to Cliff Branch. He also scored a touchdown by first blocking a blitzing linebacker, then sliding off and circling out of the backfield to take a pass from Plunkett, then dancing past two tacklers to the end zone. The Raiders easily won the game over the Falcons, 38–14. But then came the threatened strike. Marcus had rolled up 172 yards rushing, fourth best in the conference, and had caught eight passes for 103 yards. Now he, like the rest of the players in the NFL, would have to wait to see if there would be a season at all. Finally, after 57 days, the strike ended. With the season now reduced to seven more games, the Raiders went into the Coliseum to take on the San Diego Chargers. Marcus's former "hometown" team rolled up a 24–0 first-half lead, but the Raiders, with Marcus scoring two touchdowns in the third quarter, came back to take the game, 28–24!

In the next game the Raiders lost to the powerful Cincinnati Bengals, 31–17, and Marcus, although catching six passes for 54 yards, was held to no yards on eight carries. For consolation Marcus turned to his old friend, O.J., who told him he was once held to *minus*-ten yards. When Marcus told O.J., "At least I broke even," they both laughed.

In the next game Marcus returned to form and made a couple of long runs—33 and 53 yards—to help nail the Seattle Seahawks, 28–23. In all, he had rushed for 156 yards and scored two touchdowns. The Raiders managed to beat the Chiefs in Kansas City, 21–16, even though Marcus was held to 47 yards. Then, in what was billed the Battle of Los Angeles, the Raiders took on the Los Angeles Rams. Again Marcus showed his talents by running for 93 yards and scoring three touchdowns. He also caught eight passes for 61 yards in helping the Raiders to a 37–31 win and a spot in the upcoming playoffs.

In the final two games of the season, against Denver and San Diego, Marcus helped the Raiders to boost their short-season record to 8–1. In the final game, a wild 41–34 victory, Marcus gained 126 yards and scored two touchdowns. It was the kind of performance which caused Coach Flores, himself the first Raiders quarterback back in 1960, to proclaim, "There is no question that God blessed us by giving us Marcus Allen."

In the first round of the playoffs the Raiders took on the New York Jets before 90,000 fans in the Coliseum, but despite a four-yard touchdown run by Marcus in the second half, which put the Raiders on top 14–10, the Jets came back to take the game 17–14 on a 45-yard TD pass from Richard Todd to Wesley Walker.

Marcus and the Raiders would have to wait another year. But the team had returned to respectability, and for Marcus, who finished the year with 697 yards and a league-leading 11 touchdowns on the ground and three receiving, there was one last consolation. The Raiders' newest superstar had won the offensive Rookie of the Year award! He was also selected to the All-Pro team and just happened to be the first rookie nonkicker since Hall of Famer Gale Sayers, the former great runner for the Chicago Bears, to lead the league in scoring (84 points).

It seemed that all the scouts who thought Marcus wasn't big or fast enough to play in the NFL had to go back to check their computer printouts.

4
The Longest Touchdown

As the new 1983 NFL season dawned, the Raiders had proved that they were able to survive the move to their new home in Los Angeles by finishing the strike season with an 8–1 record. They had also unveiled the league's newest triple-threat running back sensation in Marcus Allen. But a loss to the Jets in the playoff round had proved that the team had not returned to the form that had brought them a victory in the 1981 Super Bowl which followed the 1980 season. Also, and more importantly, Marcus's ability in pro ball was now known. No longer would opposing teams be caught off guard. They would design their defenses to stop him, and that meant that they would be "keying" on him with at least one defender always in pursuit, whether he had the ball or not.

Still, in the opening game against the Bengals in Cincinnati, Marcus scored two touchdowns in leading the Raiders to a 20–10 victory. In that game he was held to 47 yards in 17 carries. Then, in the next game, against the Houston Oilers back at the Coliseum, Marcus gained 96 yards in a 20–6 victory. It was a marked improvement for Marcus, who once again got to carry the ball 17 times.

In the next two games the Raiders were to beat Miami, 27–14, and Denver, 22–7, to run their record to 4–0. Marcus had rushed for 105 yards against the Dolphins, but was held to 45 yards by the Broncos. The Raiders then went into Washington to play the defending Super Bowl champion Redskins. As Marcus sat out his first game because of a bruised hip, quarterback Joe Theismann and running back John Riggins helped give Washington the win in a wild 37–35 affair. Aside from losing the game, the Raiders also lost the services of wide receiver Cliff Branch, who pulled a hamstring muscle on a 99-yard touchdown play. With Branch out of action the Raiders' long passing threat was gone and the pressure increased on Marcus. Teams could now concentrate more on stopping the run.

The Raiders returned home to edge Kansas City, 21–20, as Marcus returned to the lineup. He was only able to rush for 53 yards, but gained 58 yards as a receiver and 49 yards as a passer. One of those passes, a 21-yard strike to Dokie Williams, resulted in a touchdown. In the fourth quarter the Raiders were down 20–14, and it took a recovery by Marcus of a Raider fumble in the end zone to ensure the victory. Marcus's comments after the game told of his determination to win: "I hadn't been in the end zone in some time. I had to get there one way or the other."

Marcus had now gained 346 yards after six games, but the spotlight in the AFC now had to be shared by rookie Curt Warner of the Seattle Seahawks, who led the conference with 531 yards. The spotlight in Los Angeles was also no longer the sole possession of Marcus. Not only had John Robinson, his coach at USC, taken over as head coach of the Rams, but there was another outstanding rookie running back on the loose by the name of Erik Dickerson, who had run up a total of 787 yards. But, in all fairness to Marcus, he was given the ball far less. And the Rams designed their offense around Dickerson, while the Raiders still relied on a passing game. Marcus, in fact, was only getting to carry the ball an average of 15 times a game, less than half of what he was used to in college.

In the next game, the Seahawks upended the Raiders, 38–36, with Marcus running for 86 yards. The Raiders recovered to beat Dallas 40–38 when substitute quarterback Marc Wilson passed for 318 yards and threw for three touchdowns. Marcus did not have a good game, rushing for 55 yards on 15 carries and fumbling twice, once to set up a Cowboys field goal. Marcus also had trouble in the next game, as he was held to 30 yards on the ground and fumbled to set up a Seahawks touchdown. The final score was 34–21, with the Seahawks on top. But Marcus and the Raiders recovered their winning habits and took the title in the AFC West with a 12–4 mark.

Marcus could feel good about finishing the season with over 1,000 yards on the ground (1,014) and 590 yards as a receiver, but there wasn't much time for feeling good. The playoffs were about to start. Marcus had a strong game against the Steelers with 121 yards—highlighted by a 49-yard TD run—to help the Raiders to a 38–10 victory. Now the Raiders would have to take on the troublesome Seahawks, who had beaten them twice in the regular season, in the AFC championship game. This time, though, Marcus and the Raiders were ready. Marcus gained a personal season-high 154 yards on the ground and 62 on the receiving end. The Raiders also gave Warner a taste of the same medicine that Marcus had been getting all year. They "keyed" on Warner and held him to 26 yards as the Raiders headed for Super Bowl XVIII with an impressive 30–10 win.

As the Raiders moved on to Tampa Bay, Florida, for their meeting with the Redskins, who had gone through the season with a 16–2 record, the best in football, most of the talk centered on John Riggins, the Redskins' powerful running back. Not only had

Riggins rushed for a record 166 yards in last year's Super Bowl win over Miami, 27–17, and carried off the MVP game honors, but he had scored 24 touchdowns rushing during the regular season, a new NFL record! And while Theismann was the crowd favorite and field general for the Redskins, the Raiders had to rely on quarterback Jim Plunkett, who had come off the bench in the tenth game to replace the injured Marc Wilson. Naturally, the Redskins were favored to win.

As the game began before a crowd of 72,920, the winds at Tampa Stadium were strong. It would be a problem for the quarterbacks to throw deep, and the ground game became even more important. There was no scoring until late in the first quarter when Derrick Jensen, captain of the Raiders' special teams, recovered a blocked punt in the end zone. Washington came back with a field goal in the second quarter to make the score 7–3. Plunkett then connected with Cliff Branch to run the score to 14–3. With the half coming to a close, Washington had the ball on its 12-yard line when Lyle Alzado, a great defensive end, intercepted a Theismann pass and ran it in for a commanding 21–3 lead.

If the first half belonged to the Raiders' defense, the second half belonged to Marcus Allen. Riggins moved the Redskins back into the game following a 70-yard drive which cut the lead to 21–9 (the extra-point attempt was blocked). Then Marcus took over. Plunkett completed a series of short passes and Marcus gained chunks of yards with his slashing runs. With the ball on the five-yard line Marcus took it in to cap a 70-yard drive and send the score to 28–9. What came next was pure excitement. After Washington failed to score, the Raiders got the ball on their 26-yard line. Plunkett handed off to Marcus. He started wide and then cut back inside. Before any of the defenders could react he broke free and raced downfield. The electrified crowd was on their feet and screaming as Marcus crossed the end line and scored. It was a 74-yard run, the longest in Super Bowl history!

Marcus's exciting run took the last bit of steam out of the Redskins. When the game was over, the 38–9 score demonstrated without a doubt that the underdog Raiders were the better team. Marcus, with a Super Bowl record 191 yards on 20 carries, was selected as the MVP of the game. Riggins had been held to only 64 yards on 26 carries.

Even President Ronald Reagan was impressed. He called and congratulated the team and especially Marcus. He jokingly told Marcus that the Russians had called insisting that Marcus was a "secret weapon" that should be dismantled. As to Marcus's own reaction to what was the biggest day in his young football life, he said: "This is the icing on the cake. The Heisman Trophy was an award I'll cherish, but the Super Bowl is a team goal. I just happened to make some big plays. I don't think I've ever had a bigger game in a significant game like this. This is a different level. This is number one. This is an extravaganza. Records are made to be broken, but I'm going to enjoy these for a while."

When Marcus was reminded by reporters about how earlier in the season he complained to owner Al Davis that he wasn't doing enough running and Davis told him to jog after practice, he remarked with a smile, "Mr. Davis said he was saving me for the playoffs."

5

Coming Back to Earth

For most teams who win the Super Bowl, the following year seems to be a return to reality. After all, every team plays a little harder against the Super Bowl winner. The Raiders were no exception to this fact of life. In winning Super Bowl XVIII the Raiders had won their third title in eight seasons. They were second in overall wins to the Pittsburgh Steelers, who had won four titles and had also lost once, to the Green Bay Packers, way back in Super Bowl II.

The team got off to a good start in the 1984 season with consecutive victories over Houston, Green Bay, Kansas City, and San Diego, but then they went into Mile High Stadium to play Denver and lost 16–13. Although they recovered to reel off wins against Seattle, Minnesota, and San Diego, they ran into a string of three straight losses that was an omen of things to come. Denver beat them again, this time by a 22–19 score, and they lost in Chicago by 17–6. The three-game losing streak was completed by Seattle, who beat the Raiders 17–14.

With the Raiders' record at 7–4, they came back with wins over Kansas City, Indianapolis (which had moved from Baltimore), Miami, and Detroit. In the Miami game Marcus Allen provided the highlight as he rushed for 155 yards—his season high—against the Super Bowl–bound Dolphins. The Raiders then lost the regular-season closer to Pittsburgh, 13–7, to put their final record at 11–5–0. Of the five losses, three came on the road. The team did manage to qualify for the playoffs but were eliminated 13–7 by the Seahawks. Considering what the previous year had brought, 1984 was a disappointing season.

Most of the problems could be found at the quarterback position, where a lack of mobility by Marc Wilson and Jim Plunkett resulted in 49 sacks. Both were also the victims of interceptions, with Wilson accounting for 17 and Plunkett for ten. Only Marcus, with his second straight 1,000-yard season, could claim any real victory. He had caught 64 passes for 758 yards, more than any other running back in the AFC. He also shared the league lead with 18 touchdowns and 108 points with Miami's Mark Clayton! The 18 TDs set a new Raiders team record. But it wasn't enough to overcome a mediocre team showing. Also, the conference rushing title was lost to San Diego's Earnest Jackson by a 1,179 to 1,168 margin (11 yards). Jackson, by the way, got the ball 296 times compared to Marcus's 275.

To add fuel to the fire, Marcus had fallen in the shadow of Los Angeles's Eric Dickerson. The Rams' talented running back had broken O. J. Simpson's season record by rushing for a staggering 2,105 yards! The small detail of Dickerson's carrying the ball over 100 times more than Marcus (379 to 275) was mostly ignored by the press, as was the fact that Dickerson isn't noted for his blocking or receiving skills. It was the kind of situation which sportswriters dream about, inventing a rivalry where none really exists. Perhaps to listen to Marcus's own comments on Dickerson and the Raiders' season best gives the inside story: "People said I was jealous of Eric, that I was sulking because of his success. I can honestly tell you I wasn't jealous at all. But after the season I sat down and reflected on my three years in the league and reevaluated what I wanted to achieve personally, and some things just weren't as important. I said to myself, 'Listen, I don't have to lead the league in rushing and receiving and blocking, too. If the yards come, fine.'

"I considered our [team] philosophy. Pass first, then run. It isn't geared to rushing titles. Now it's changed, through necessity. Jim Plunkett's out, Marc Wilson's been beat up every week. The load just fell on me. I feel I'm running differently now. Last year [1984] I was pressing. I was impatient. I wasn't allowing the offense to develop in front of me. I was leaving the blockers and free-lancing. People would tell me I was doing well, but actually I was just coming close and not really getting there."

Because Marcus is someone who strives for perfection, he may have been a bit too critical of his own performance. A better idea of Marcus's contribution to the Raiders came from John Mackovic, coach of the AFC rival Kansas City Chiefs, when he said, "Marcus has a great feel and vision for what's going on. He's a great competitor. He does not like to be denied yardage. If it's third-and-three and they give him the ball, he's going to get the three. If it's first-and-ten he wants ten, not three or four [yards]. When they're on the goal line, he walks on people's backs to get into the end zone. He wants whatever there is to get."

As it turned out, there were still plenty of goals and awards for Marcus to focus on. And 1985 would add more luster to his brilliant career.

6

The Player of the Year

Marcus Allen went into the 1985 season with a brand-new contract from the Raiders' management. After proving since his arrival three years before that he was the best offensive weapon the team had ever had, Marcus was awarded with a five-year, three-and-a-half-million-dollar contract! And even more than the money, it was a vote of confidence that he was indeed one of the true superstars of the NFL.

It was enough of a boost to give Marcus the confidence to have the best year of his pro career and to set some more records, too. In the first regular-season game Marcus rushed for 76 yards, caught passes for 30 yards, and completed one 16-yard pass as the Raiders blanked the Jets 31–0 to record their first shutout since 1977. The team then traveled to Kansas City and were beaten 36–20 as Marcus was given the ball only 14 times and rushed for a lowly 50 yards.

In the third game of the season the Raiders took on the defending Super Bowl champion San Francisco 49ers and were beaten 34–10 before the first sellout crowd in the Raiders' short history in the Coliseum. This time Marcus was given the ball only 12 times but still managed to rush for a respectable 59 yards. On the receiving end he caught eight passes for 53 yards.

The Raiders were in real trouble in the next game when they lost the services of quarterbacks Jim Plunkett and Marc Wilson due to injuries. Coach Tom Flores had to make some drastic changes. Instead of relying on long, TD-type passes and a freewheeling offense, he decided to have the team concentrate on defense and ball control. He also decided to call the plays. For Marcus, who had been averaging 17 carries a game for the past three years, it meant getting the ball and carrying it an average of 27 times a game. The difference was like taking an instant health cure.

In that injury-plagued game Marcus got the ball 21 times against the Patriots in New England and rushed for 98 yards. He also caught three passes for 30 yards as the Raiders came from behind to win 35–20. Marcus had some unexpected scoring help from 260-pound Lyle Alzado, who recovered a fumble for a touchdown and scored two other points on a safety.

In the next game, against Kansas City, the Raiders won 19–10 as Marcus carried the ball a career-high 29 times and finished the day with 126 rushing yards. New Orleans then came into the Coliseum and Marcus rushed for 107 yards in a 23–13 victory. He also caught three passes for 51 yards and scored two touchdowns. With the team record now at 4–2, the Raiders went into Cleveland to play the Browns and won 21–20 in the last minute of play. Marcus gained 81 yards on the ground and 41 through the air. He also scored a touchdown.

Marcus then started a string of 100-yard-plus games which put his name in the record books ahead of his pal, O. J. Simpson, and Earl Campbell and tied him with the great Walter Payton of the Chicago Bears. In games against San Diego, Seattle, and San Diego again, Marcus turned in rushing performances of 111, 101, and 119 yards. But the Raiders could only split with San Diego, losing the second game in over-time, and they could not overcome the Kingdome jinx against the Seahawks. It also was the first time the Raiders had lost when Allen rushed for 100 yards.

The team record was 5–4, and another loss would certainly put them out of the playoff picture. The Bengals came to town, and Marcus gained 189 of the Raiders' 284 yards, 135 on the ground, as the Raiders won 13–6. But in that game defensive end Alzado tore an Achilles tendon which ended his career. It took an overtime win against Denver, 31–28, to keep the Raiders in the race. In the game Marcus rushed for a regular-season career high of 173 yards, 61 of them coming on a run much like the one which had brought him a record in the Super Bowl. His rushing yardage for the day marked the 14th time he had accomplished 100 yards during a regular-season game and tied the team record held by Mark van Eeghen.

The Raiders were now 7–4 and Marcus had five consecutive games of 100 or more yards rushing. The team went into Atlanta and won 34–24 as Marcus carried the ball 28 times for 156 yards. He not only surpassed van Eeghen's all-time season mark with his total of 1,392 yards but took over the league lead in rushing, a fact that didn't mean that much to Marcus. "The most important thing to come out of the game was the fact that we won. The fact that I took the lead in rushing is not the important thing. Leading the league isn't as important to me now as it was when I first came into the league."

After winning 17–14 in overtime at Denver, where Marcus gained 135 yards in spite of a special four-man line to stop him, an odd thing happened. The Raiders beat Seattle as Marcus rushed for 109 yards—his eighth straight game of 100 yards—but instead of tying the all-time NFL record held by Simpson and Campbell, he only got to share an old record because Walter Payton was recording his ninth straight 100-yard game during the same week! In the last game of the season, against the Rams and Eric Dickerson,

Marcus tied Payton as the Jets' strong defense stopped the mighty Chicago running back from extending his streak while Marcus rushed for 123 yards. The Raiders also won the game, 16–6, and finished the season with a 12–4 mark. For the third time in the past four years they were the winners of the AFC Western Division. For Marcus, it was an incredible year. His 1,759 yards was the best in the league, and his combined yardage from scrimmage (rushing and receiving) of 2,314 yards established a new NFL record! His 14 touchdowns and 84 points were second in the league to Pittsburgh's exciting wide receiver, Louis Lipps.

Before the Raiders took on New England in the playoffs, Marcus was watching another conference game when he learned that no one who had ever won a rushing title had ever won a Super Bowl in the same year. It wasn't a good omen. As things turned out, Marcus never even got a chance to go to the Super Bowl. New England, which would play its way to the championship game, upset the Raiders 27–20. For Marcus there was no shame as he rushed for 121 yards. But there was disappointment. Not winning was the important thing. As he said, "At the outset of each year, the measurement you use is going to the Super Bowl. While the awards are special, they're no consolation for not going to the Super Bowl."

Fortunately, Marcus wasn't going to vote on who was the Most Valuable Player in the league. Chances are he wouldn't have voted for himself. But enough people did to bring him the 1985 *Sporting News* Marlboro Player of the Year Award as well as the Schick Trophy for being selected the MVP by the Professional Football Writers Association. Also, with teammates Todd Christensen, a tight end, Howie Long, a defensive end, and Mike Haynes, a cornerback, Marcus was selected to the All-Pro team. As a final topper, he and Howie Long were honored in Miami by Seagram's as the league's top offensive and defensive players.

Long, by the way, had nominated Marcus for league MVP at midseason. After the season was over, he said, "What can you say about the man? He's probably the toughest man I know. If he's not the MVP of the league, I don't know who is." Raiders linebacker Matt Millen joined in the praise: "He's the MVP if I ever saw one. There can't be anybody in the league who has meant so much to one team as Marcus has meant to ours. Because if you take away Allen from our offense, you basically have nothing."

And to think that Marcus, who has been called the Artful Raider, still has thousands of yards and years to go before he hangs up his magic running shoes.

STATISTICS

JIM McMAHON
6' 0" 187 lbs., born August 21, 1959
attended Brigham Young University

1985 Quarterback Rating

Completions	Attempts	%	Total Yards
178	313	56.9	2,392

Average Gain	TDs	TD 0/0	INT	INT 0/0	Rating
7.64	15	4.8	11	3.5	82.6

NFL Regular Season Passing Statistics

Year	Comp.	Att.	Yards	Avg.	TDs
1982	120	210	1,501	7.15	9
1983	175	295	2,184	7.40	12
1984	85	143	1,146	8.01	8
1985	178	313	2,392	7.64	15
Totals	558	961	7,223	7.52	44

MARCUS ALLEN
6' 2" 205 lbs., born March 26, 1960
attended University of Southern California

NFL Regular Season Rushing Statistics

Year	Att.	Yards	Avg.	TDs
1982	160	697	4.4	11
1983	266	1,014	3.8	9
1984	275	1,168	4.2	13
1985	380	1,759	4.6	11
Totals	1,081	4,638	4.3	44

NFL Regular Season Pass Receiving Statistics

Year	Passes Caught	Yards	Avg.	TDs
1982	38	401	10.6	3
1983	68	590	8.7	2
1984	64	758	11.8	5
1985	67	555	8.3	3
Totals	237	2,304	9.7	13

JIM McMAHON

College Statistics

Rushing

Year	Comp.	Att.	Yards	Avg.	TDs
1978	87	176	1,307	7.43	6
1979			did not play		
1980	284	445	4,571*	10.27	47
1981	272	423	3,555	8.40	30
Totals	643	1,044	9,433	9.05	83

*NCAA record

MARCUS ALLEN

College Statistics

Rushing

Year	Att.	Yards	Avg.	TDs
1978	31	171	5.5	1
1979	114	649	5.7	8
1980	354	1,563	4.4	14
1981	433	2,427	5.6	22
Totals	932	4,810	5.2	45

Pass Receiving

Years	Passes Caught	Yards	Avg.	TDs
1978	0	0	0	0
1979	22	314	14.3	0
1980	30	231	7.7	0
1981	34	256	7.5	1
Totals	86	801	9.3	1